Original title:
Woodland Wanderlust

Copyright © 2025 Creative Arts Management OÜ
All rights reserved.

Author: Riley Donovan
ISBN HARDBACK: 978-1-80567-225-8
ISBN PAPERBACK: 978-1-80567-524-2

The Call of the Rustic Realm

In a forest where squirrels do dance,
I tripped on a root and lost my pants.
The birds laughed, oh what a sight,
As I chased my shorts in pure delight.

Mushrooms whispered secrets quite absurd,
While a rabbit joined in, it seemed disturbed.
A raccoon chuckled as I passed by,
Clearly, my fashion choice made him sigh.

Enchantment Among the Roots

Beneath a tree, I found a frog,
Who croaked a tune, all smug as a dog.
I joined in, both off-key and bold,
It turned the woods into tales retold.

A squirrel with sunglasses watched my show,
He tapped his paw, putting on a glow.
"Bravo!" he shouted, leading the cheer,
Until a branch fell, and I disappeared!

Gazing at Thickets of Time

I stared at bushes, quite profound,
Wondering if my lunch was around.
A hedgehog peeked out, quite curious too,
With spines that glistened like morning dew.

We held a meeting, the hedgehog and I,
Discussing if mushrooms could learn to fly.
The thicket giggled at our grand schemes,
As we plotted to wake up the dreams.

The Aroma of Earth and Sky

I sniffed the air, oh what a blend,
Of dampened leaves and a bug's rear end.
The scent of pine made me sneeze three times,
While a raccoon remixed nature's chimes.

A fox in a top hat strolled by with flair,
"Do you smell that?" he said, "It's debonair!"
And deeper we went into foliage bright,
Searching for snacks, oh what a delight!

Secrets in the Forest Shadows

In shadows deep, where squirrels plot,
They toss acorns like they've won the lot.
A mischievous fox grins with delight,
As a raccoon steals the popcorn at night.

Mushrooms giggle in the dappled sun,
Their polka dots make mushrooms fun.
Listen close; secrets float in the air,
Like lost socks in the dryer — beware!

The owls hoot jokes, but they're really sly,
Feigning wisdom while watching passersby.
Wisecracks echo through the bark and twig,
Turning shy deer into jiggy pigs!

If you tread softly past misty glade,
You might find a party where all are laid.
Join the sprites in their moonlit caper,
You just might leave with magic paper!

Journey Through the Gnarled Roots

Through tangled threads of ancient trees,
I hop like I'm swatting at buzzing bees.
Twisting paths beneath the leafy walls,
Even lost squirrels watch as I trip and fall.

The roots invite, like a stretch from bed,
But one caught my shoe — it resembles Fred!
Again I stumble, then burst into laughter,
Nature's dance floors are a perfect disaster.

Weaving tales with each winding stride,
The trees are witnesses to my wild ride.
A chipmunk heckles, I'm lost in jest,
"Can't you find your way? You know the rest!"

At last, I find a sign, scrawled with cheer,
Directions taken? I'm still nowhere near.
Yet joy's in the journey, oh what a sight,
With berries and laughter, the day feels right!

A Symphony of Rustling Leaves

Leaves rustle softly, a symphonic sound,
As if they're gossiping all around.
Each step I take adds to their song,
Together we dance, it's never wrong.

The breeze whispers secrets, oh what a tease,
Be careful, it might tickle your knees.
A frog joins in with a naval croak,
While ants perform, all wearing a cloak.

Beneath a twirling cloud of fluff,
I trip on the roots – is that really tough?
But laughter erupts, there's magic in play,
With every tumble, I'm led astray.

The sun dips low, the concert's a dream,
Join in with the critters, or so it seems.
For as they rustle, they tempt and tease,
Join in their chorus with joyful ease!

The Silhouette of Twilight Trees

When twilight whispers secrets and sighs,
The trees cast shadows that dance and rise.
A raccoon in a top hat, oh what a sight,
Lurking beneath the gentle moonlight.

With branches like arms, they sway left and right,
As I try to mimic their elegant flight.
But tripping over roots feels like ballet,
These woods are quite playful, come join the fray!

Bats swoop in with a hilarious buzz,
Dancing like they're all part of a fuzz.
"Catch me if you can!" they chirp and flit,
While I gasp for breath, feeling quite unfit.

Yet here in the dusk, laughter prevails,
As I weave through trees with ridiculous tales.
These silhouettes of fun, they light up the night,
With every chuckle, I take joyful flight!

Beneath the Arching Branches

Beneath the arching branches wide,
The squirrels plot their secret stride.
They chatter loud, all full of glee,
While birds roll eyes as if to plea.

A rabbit pranks a sleepy hare,
Who wakes up startled, pulls at air.
The mushrooms giggle in a row,
As nature's antics steal the show.

The Language of Leaves and Wind

The leaves debate in whispers sweet,
While breezes dance on tiny feet.
A dandelion gets advice,
From acorns rolling, oh so nice!

The wind tells jokes, a chuckle flies,
As clouds above join in the guise.
With puffs and purls, they drift and sway,
In laughter shared, they spend the day.

Trails of Secrets and Serenity

On trails where secrets loop and twine,
The critters gossip, feeling fine.
A deer forgot its way to graze,
And ends up stuck in leafy maze.

A fox, bemused, just takes a seat,
While turtles slowly shuffle, greet.
All watch the chaos, hoots and growls,
Laughing at the lost one's prowls.

Beneath the Eaves of an Ancient Oak

Beneath the eaves where shadows play,
A cheeky raccoon leads the way.
He swipes a snack with nimble grace,
While startled owls just shake their face.

The oak whispers tales of days gone past,
As squirrels rush with nuts amassed.
In giggles, echoes fill the air,
With every rustle, laughter's share.

Underneath the Green-touched Sky

Beneath the leaves, I tripped and fell,
A squirrel laughed, oh, do tell!
My compass spun like a dancing spree,
Lost again—I'll never be free!

The mushrooms wink with a cheeky grin,
Join the party, let the chaos begin!
A raccoon juggles acorns with delight,
Even the pinecones join in the fight!

Chasing shadows, I find a friend,
A tree stump whispers, "This is the end!"
I wave goodbye with a jesting shout,
But off I wander, no doubt about!

So here I roam, in nature's jest,
Each misstep becomes a quest.
With laughter echoing through the trees,
I'll keep wandering, if you please!

When the Woodlands Speak

The oaks are chatting, it's quite absurd,
They gossip loudly, every word.
I stood and listened, made quite a fuss,
"Is that a rumor?" I asked a bus!

The ferns all giggled, in sacred glee,
"Here comes that fool, just let it be!"
I bowed politely, though I felt a fool,
While squirrels debated who was most cool.

A pine cone asked, "What's your great plan?"
"To find some snacks, if I can!"
Then off they scampered, quite quick and spry,
Leaving me chuckling beneath the sky.

In this woodsy whirl, I find my bliss,
With all this chatter, how could I miss?
As whispers dance on the breeze like a song,
I'm tethered to laughter, it's where I belong!

Treading the Trails of Time

I marched along, with gusto and glee,
"Look at me, world, wild and free!"
A twig snapped loudly! I jumped in fright,
Turns out it was just a frog taking flight.

Tick-tock tickled by shadows so sly,
My watch is a compass—a very bad lie!
Each step a giggle, each stumble a cheer,
I ask the trees, "Hey, where's the beer?"

With every step, I lose more grace,
A tumble, a roll—what a comical race!
The trail twists like a winding joke,
Nature giggles at each silly poke.

So here I trample with all my clout,
In paths where laughter blooms all about.
With every misstep, a story to share,
In this enchanted realm, with no care!

The Cloak of Forest Fantasies

Draped in leaves, I feel so grand,
A crown of twigs, oh, isn't it planned?
The forest chuckles as I prance,
A bearded tree asks me to dance!

With acorns for shoes, I skip with flair,
Each rustle a giggle, a whisper of air.
A fox in a suit joins the bizarre fête,
"Let's toast to the trees! We might be late!"

Glowing mushrooms twinkle like stars aglow,
"Come join our party, we've got quite the show!"
"Is this a dream?" I ponder with zest,
"Or have I been jesting? Am I truly blessed?"

So I twirl in laughter under emerald beams,
Where nature's humor fuels silly dreams.
With every step, I lose and I find,
In this magical place, I'm delightfully blind!

Ferns and Fables Beneath the Boughs

In the shade of leafy friends,
I tripped on roots and laughed,
A squirrel stole my sandwich fast,
Now I'm on a leafy raft.

With tales spun by buzzing bees,
And chatter from the chirpy throng,
The brambles play their sneaky tricks,
As I stumble through the ferns so strong.

The mushrooms wink with glee,
As I dance with a daffodil,
Oh, the world of whims and charms,
How I love this nature thrill!

A frog in boots hops by with flair,
He tips his hat and gives a grin,
In this wild and wacky place,
Even the trees have cheeky kin!

Where the Wildflowers Dream

Where daisies wear hats made of dew,
And tulips gossip with a sway,
Bees form bands in shades of blue,
While petals waltz the day away.

With colors splashed like painter's glee,
I joined the dance of blooms so bright,
But tripped on grass, oh, the irony!
What's a dance without a little fright?

A butterfly with comical grace,
Played tag with blooms in vibrant rows,
While I just tried to keep the pace,
And dodge a buzz from nosy crows.

As blooms conspire in evening light,
I laugh at their fragrant schemes,
For in this garden full of delight,
I've found a realm of wild dreams!

Echoes of the Ancient Grove

In the heart of timeless trees,
Whispers giggle and sneak around,
I swear I heard an oak say,
'Can we keep the squirrels unbound?'

The ancient roots twist and snake,
As shadows play a game of tag,
With ferns that bow and trees that quake,
My laughter echoes, never drab.

A hedgehog juggles acorns high,
While raccoons plan a midnight feast,
I watch with wide and silly eyes,
Wondering who's the wackiest beast!

Together we weave fables old,
With every step, more tales unfold,
For nature's giggles, bright and bold,
Keep our spirits forever sold.

Starlit Reveries in the Thicket

Underneath the twinkling lights,
Glow worms host a starlit show,
I tried to join their funny rites,
But tripped on roots and fell below.

With owls hooting in delight,
And raccoons having a snack-time,
The night turned into pure delight,
As I clumsily joined their rhyme.

Crickets chirp, a silly tune,
As fireflies match a sparkler's fizz,
Laughter shines beneath the moon,
In this cuddly woodland whiz.

So let's embrace this midnight spree,
Where mischief reigns and joy is free,
In the thicket, wild and spry,
We dance with spirits 'neath the sky!

The Dance of the Dappled Sunlight

In the glade where shadows play,
The sunbeams tease the leaves all day,
A squirrel tries a twirl and spin,
As if he's dancing with the wind.

A rabbit hops with quite a flair,
While hedgehogs stop to stop and stare,
The ladybugs in tiny boots,
Start swaying to the earthy roots.

Now come the frogs, with leaps so high,
They croak a tune, oh my, oh my!
A turtle joins, not quite in sync,
But not to care, no time to think.

So join the fun within this space,
Where nature hosts a happy race,
With every creature on display,
In the dappled sun's ballet.

Pathways of Green and Gold

Down winding trails both wide and narrow,
A snail's adventure, quite grand, not feral,
He leaves a trail, it's quite a sight,
As leafy snacks delay his flight.

The ants march in a tiny band,
Their picnic blankets close at hand,
A crumb they find, oh what a feast,
Go on, my friends, you're quite the beast!

A chipmunk yells from high above,
With acorns dropped, it's like a shove,
While deer tiptoe like in a game,
"Who stole my snack?" oh what a shame!

So stroll along this vibrant lane,
Watch every creature, none in vain,
For every step is filled with cheer,
In green and gold, it's crystal clear.

Enchanted Echoes of the Underbrush

Within the bushes, whispers creep,
With chatty birds who never sleep,
A fox eavesdrops and starts to grin,
At tales of mischief, where to begin?

A raccoon sneaks a late-night snack,
His "stealth mode" really lacks a knack,
He bumps and tumbles, what a sight,
In moonlit chaos, pure delight!

The owls hoot with such great flair,
"Who's up for a midnight scare?"
They swoop down low, a funny sight,
Making all creatures take flight!

So wander through this lively wood,
Where echoes crack with fun when they should,
Nature's laughter fills the air,
An underbrush with tales to share.

The Hidden Stream's Lullaby

Beneath the boughs, a stream does gurgle,
With pebbles swirling, dance and burble,
A frog conducts with great finesse,
While fish perform, oh what a mess!

A beaver tries to build a dam,
But slips and splashes—what a scam!
The ducks quack loudly in disdain,
"Come help us out, we're in the rain!"

An otter rolls, quite suave indeed,
With acorn hats he's made for speed,
And salmon bump the banks with pride,
"Come join us, buddy, for a ride!"

So listen close, oh wandering friend,
To nature's tune that will not end,
For laughter bubbles in each wave,
In hidden streams, joy's what we crave.

Green Labyrinths of Beauty and Mystery

In the forest where the squirrels dare,
Trees wear hats, so debonair.
A rabbit with a monocle grins,
As mushrooms giggle, each one spins.

The bushes play hide and seek,
With all the critters, bold and cheek.
A fox in slippers, oh what a sight,
Bouncing through leaves, pure delight!

The paths twist like a winding maze,
Where gnomes have their nightly plays.
A caper of raccoons, what a scene,
Cracking jokes, oh so keen!

With every turn, more laughs arise,
As owls hoot their silly cries.
In this place, joy's the only quest,
Nature's chuckle is truly the best.

Heartbeats in the Hushed Hollow

In a hollow where the crickets sing,
The trees wear crowns, oh what a fling!
A turtle dashes, oh such a tease,
While chipmunks twirl in the cool breeze.

A chorus of leaves is a funky tune,
With butterflies dancing under the moon.
A bear tap dances, quite out of time,
While the fireflies glow, a light so prime.

A bumblebee's buzz is a trumpet's call,
As ants put on a show, standing tall.
The shadows twist, making funny shapes,
Even the rocks wear silly capes!

In this hollow, hearts skip and hum,
As laughter bounces like a bongo drum.
The rhythm of joy makes everything right,
In the hush of the night, life's pure delight.

The Chronicle of Twilight Walks

Under twilight's gentle glow,
Trees gossip, as breezes blow.
A hedgehog with a top hat struts,
While fireflies shine and twinkle, what a fuss!

The mushrooms form a band, they play,
A beetle croons, in a jazzy way.
A raccoon in shades, so smooth and spring,
Chasing after notes, with sweet zing!

A toad on a log is the DJ's guide,
While frogs leap like they're on a ride.
With shadows dancing, laughter spills,
As the woods echo, with joyful thrills.

Every step is like a festive parade,
With tiny footprints that never fade.
Among the twinkles and sighs, we find,
The secret happiness woven and twined.

Tracing Echoes of Ethereal Light

In the glimmers of twilight so bright,
The trees hold secrets, oh what a sight!
A fox whispers tales of enchanted quest,
While owls wear glasses, not allowing rest.

Stars sprinkle laughter across the sky,
As ladybugs spin, oh my, oh my!
A dance of shadows, a playful bid,
With playful giggles from every hid.

The brook chuckles, tickling the vine,
While hedgies hum a soothing line.
With sprightly steps on the woodland floor,
Nature's giggle invites us to explore.

As echoes ripple, joy takes flight,
We'll follow the fun in the soft moonlight.
Adventure sings in the whispers of night,
As we trace echoes of pure delight.

Secrets Held in the Bark

Tree stumps hold secrets grand,
Of squirrels with acorn plans.
Bark whispers tales of the past,
Of moments fleeting and fast.

A raccoon with a mask quite sly,
Steals snacks as he scurries by.
The owls hoot jokes from their roost,
While ants march on, feeling too spruced.

Saplings gossip, oh so spry,
As beetles dance, oh me, oh my!
Each twig a tricky little tease,
Nature's antics, always sure to please.

So next time you wander fair,
Join the laugh, breathe in the air.
For in the woods, giggles resonate,
In every leaf and fallen crate.

Trails of Tomorrow

Paths twist like a written riddle,
Hikers mumble, 'This is a fiddle!'
Lost my way, but what's the deal?
I'll just follow the ladybug wheel.

Beneath the vines, a frog does leap,
With a leap so grand, I drop my beep.
He croaks a tune, I can't quite catch,
Much better than my misfit scratch.

The sunlight winks through leafy crowns,
Fairies giggle, wearing crowns of browns.
'Where's the exit?' I shout with glee,
But the trees just shrug, 'Stay here, you see?'

Tomorrow's paths are filled with mirth,
Adventure blooms, glories rebirth.
So lace your shoes, let laughter flow,
In the forest of wild, let's steal the show!

Glimmers in the Underbrush

In the thickets, bright sparks shine,
The fireflies in a dance so fine.
But in a tangle, I trip and fall,
Laughter echoes, I bumble, I sprawl.

The thorns wave, 'How do you do?'
As I untangle from their goo.
With every step, a giggle grows,
Nature's pranks in playful shows.

A rabbit hops, I can't keep pace,
While mushrooms chuckle, a fungi race.
'Catch us if you can!' they tease,
Yet my feet are stuck, oh, what a wheeze!

Underbrush hides jesters of cheer,
From cheeky gnomes to badger near.
So if you wander, don't be shy,
Join the fun before you sigh.

Overlapping Canopies of Dreams

Above, the branches twist and twirl,
A canopy of secrets, it starts to swirl.
Squirrels skitter, flinging their stash,
While I dodge acorns in a frantic dash.

The canopy giggles, rich with delight,
As I play tag with shadows in flight.
Mushrooms chuckle and sway in time,
While I trip over roots, oh how sublime!

Breezes whistle silly tunes at night,
The stars wink down, sparkling bright.
'Dance with us,' the cosmos plead,
I shimmy and shake, oh, what a lead!

So look up high, and laugh out loud,
For the world's a wacky, whimsical crowd.
In every shadow, every beam,
Lies the joy of an overlapping dream.

A Dance with the Forest Spirits

In the grove of gnarled dreams,
The trees twist and sway like teams.
Mushrooms wearing tiny hats,
Invite squirrels for acrobatic chats.

A raccoon leads the merry tune,
While owls hoot at the silly moon.
Beneath the stars, the brook giggles,
As dancing frogs strike silly wiggles.

Swaying branches whisper secrets,
Of chipmunks plotting wild regrets.
Laughter echoes through the pine,
As critters sip on acorn wine.

The forest shimmies with delight,
Embracing shadows, chasing light.
With every step, the spirits prance,
In this comical forest dance.

Roaming the Realm of Roots

Roots are tangled like a joke,
Stumbling 'round, we softly poke.
Pine cones drop like shy applause,
We giggle at the tree's great pause.

Squirrels race on hidden tracks,
While laughing leaves join in the quacks.
Mighty oaks are jolly kings,
Waving branches, sharing flings.

A hedgehog scuttles, all aglow,
Chasing insects in a show.
Beneath each nook, a root-bound sprite,
Tells tales of gnomes with tiny kites.

In this realm, we skip and slide,
Where nature plays, there's joy inside.
With each misstep, a chuckled cheer,
Roots hold secrets, sweet and clear.

The Soft Footfall of Nature's Wanderers

In the thicket, whispers tease,
Foxes prance with graceful ease.
Ducks quack jokes from the stream's edge,
While rabbits hop near the green hedge.

Leaves confide in merry tones,
As badgers munch on crunchy bones.
Every footfall, a laugh-filled sigh,
As creatures scurry, wave goodbye.

A wily crow caws from high trees,
Playing pranks in the gentle breeze.
While turtles nap beneath the sun,
This woodland stroll is just pure fun.

With each soft footfall, joy unfolds,
In every wrinkle, a tale once told.
Nature's wanderers laugh and play,
A jubilant dance throughout the day.

In the Arms of Green Serenity

In the arms of trees so grand,
We find peace in nature's hand.
Laughter bubbles like a brook,
As moths read from their crinkled book.

Under branches, we kick leaves,
Playing hide and seek with thieves.
Bunnies bounce, then steal a snack,
While crafty raccoons launch a quack.

Mossy beds invite a nap,
As wildflowers make their map.
Sunshine tickles every petal,
Inviting giggles, light as metal.

With every venture, joy is stirred,
In silences, we share a word.
In green serenity, life is bright,
As nature crafts this pure delight.

Where the Wild Things Whisper

In the forest where squirrels chatter,
Leaves gossip, and branches flatter.
Hide and seek with the bumblebees,
Oh, what fun behind the trees!

The fox wears a scarf just for style,
While rabbits hop and grin with guile.
Silly raccoons hold a tea party,
Sip some dew, and act quite hearty.

The mushrooms dance in polka dot shoes,
Each step a jest, each laugh a muse.
A turtle spills tea on a mossy page,
It's a laugh riot at nature's stage!

So grab your hat, come join the spree,
In this big show of furry jubilee.
Chasing shadows and jumping puddles,
Embrace the quirkiness, no cuddles!

Driftwood Dreams in the Dappled Shade

There's a log with a grumpy old gnome,
Who swears he'll never leave his dome.
With a flip-flop hat and a snoring grunt,
He dreams of a beach while on a hunt.

The driftwood waves have stories to tell,
Like the time the sun sank into a shell.
Seagulls are planning a wild old feast,
With crabs in tuxedos, to say the least!

A raccoon thinks he's quite the chief,
Claims every twig, but we just laugh in disbelief.
The shadowy owls keep watch at night,
Making bets on who'll win the next flight!

So come take a stroll 'neath the leafy trees,
Where the chatter of critters floats on the breeze.
And if you spot any driftwood sprites,
Just wave and chuckle at their delights!

Harmonies of Hush and Harmony

In a clearing where the crickets sing,
And frogs wear hats for the upcoming fling,
They tap dance on stones, quite sprightly indeed,
While old wise turtles give sage advice with speed.

The trees are all gossiping, branches lean,
Whispers of antics that never have been seen.
A mischievous chipmunk steals acorns galore,
Dancing through shadows, always craving more!

Bubbles of laughter lift up to the sky,
While owls throw a raucous party nearby.
Each flick of a tail brings giggles and grins,
As we wade through tail tales and woodland spins!

So linger awhile, let the silence sway,
With the buzzing and humming of their own ballet.
For hidden away, in this harmony's clutch,
Lies a woodland so lively, it's all quite a punch!

The Allure of Forgotten Trails

Down a path where the squirrels strut,
And the hedgehogs grit teeth, never seem to shut.
Every step crunches with secrets untold,
While the sun weaves stories in glimmers of gold.

A bunny named Frank thinks he's quite the king,
Holding court with the bushes, and what joy they bring!
With a crown made of clover and dandelion puffs,
He hops 'round the meadow, calling all bluffs!

The path winds and twirls like a confusing joke,
Where the shadows play tag with the sun's gentle cloak.
Awash in delight, with giggles all 'round,
You'll forget what you lost, not a care to be found!

So grab your boots, lace 'em up tight,
Join the parade for a wild, laughing night.
In this quirky adventure, each trail you unveil,
Is a canvas of fun in the grand old tale!

Echoes from the Greenheart

In the trees, a squirrel chides,
As acorns drop like tiny slides.
A chipmunk cracks a nut with glee,
"Oh, look at me, I'm fancy-free!"

The leaves above gossip and weave,
Telling tales that make us believe.
A mushroom winks from the muddy ground,
"I'm the king of fungi all around!"

A rabbit hops with a silly jig,
Wearing a hat that's far too big.
The owl hoots, a plump old sage,
"Could you keep it down? I'm on a page!"

With every step, a riddle shares,
What happens when a fox declares?
"Why chase the hen, when I could dance?
Let's hold a ball, give fate a chance!"

Shadows of Sunlit Glades

A deer prances in borrowed shoes,
While the hedgehog, oh, he snoozes!
"Why wear my spines?" he snores with flair,
"When soft bedding's way more rare!"

The fireflies hum a tune at night,
"Let's flash our lights, what a sight!"
They blink their dance, like disco stars,
"Who needs a club when there's no cars?"

A raccoon steals a pie, oh dear,
"It's a feast! Come, my friends, don't fear!"
With laughter, they spill the berry blend,
A picnic party, never end!

In sunlit glades, the whispers tease,
"Stop talking trees, I'm trying to sneeze!"
The critters giggle, secrets plead,
Life in the dim doesn't need a speed!

Journey Through the Verdant Veins

The path meanders like a lazy snake,
While the frogs play leap with a grand mistake.
"Did you see that? I swear I flew!"
"Sure you did, right between the dew!"

A caterpillar in a stylish coat,
Struts with pride, he's got the float.
"What's the rush for a butterfly?"
He pauses up high, "I'm here to try!"

The clouds play peek, the sun plays fetch,
Chasing shadows, a wild sketch.
As giggles sprout from each shrub and vine,
Life is a party, oh, so divine!

Through verdant veins, let laughter ring,
What's on the menu? A new spring fling!
"Grab a twig, let's start a band,
Nature's choir in a quirky land!"

The Dance of Dappled Light

In dappled light, a party sways,
With fawns showing off their clumsy ways.
"Watch me twirl, I'm finding my groove!"
The fox laughs, "Well, you sure do move!"

The shadows stretch where sunbeams play,
And whispers float without a fray.
"Is that a dance or a funny prance?
Let's give it rhythm, and take a chance!"

A feathered friend, with a cheeky grin,
Came to join, "Where do I begin?"
With beaks and bounces, oh what a sight,
They shimmy through dusk, a pure delight!

As the day winds down, why not take flight?
"To bed," murmurs a snail, "must dim the light."
"Not yet!" chant the critters with cheer,
"Let's dance until the stars appear!"

A Journey Through Olive Shadows

In the grove where olives sway,
A squirrel mocks my clumsy way.
He darts and dives, a funny tease,
While I trip over tangled knees.

Sunlight filters through the leaves,
A chorus sings, the breeze deceives.
I dance like grass, I twist and twirl,
A squirrel rolls by—a fluffy whirl.

With every step, a story sows,
Of fruit that laughs, and nuts that pose.
A picnic spread in shady nooks,
With festive ants and laughing cooks.

At last, I sit, my treasure found,
A slice of cheese, the silliest sound.
As nature grins, I take my bite,
And giggle at my woodland plight.

Whispers Among the Pines

Amongst the pines, I hear a joke,
The wind's soft laugh, a gentle poke.
A chipmunk struts in dapper dress,
While I trip over my own stress.

They whisper secrets, oh so grand,
While nature plays a joker's hand.
I juggle pinecones, laugh at trees,
Until I sneeze and scare the bees!

The shadows dance, they poke and tease,
I trip on roots with utmost ease.
With every rustle, it's clear to see,
Even leaves have a sense of glee.

In this green world, I find delight,
With pines that giggle day and night.
My pockets stuffed with nature's quirks,
Who knew that fun was where nature lurks?

The Call of the Emerald Trail

On the emerald trail, I slide and slip,
With every step, my footing dips.
A rabbit hops, and off I chase,
But mud now decorates my face!

The ferns giggle, the flowers cheer,
As I fumble through with no great fear.
A throne of thorns, I stumble past,
I swear the bushes are laughing fast!

But lo and behold, a path appears,
Guided by chirps and whispered cheers.
With every crunch beneath my toes,
I'm the king of clumsy where the wild rose grows!

And as I dance on leaves so bright,
The forest joins in, a merry sight.
I twirl and spin, a quirky gale,
Forever bound to this cheeky trail.

Beneath the Canopy's Embrace

Beneath the canopy, I find my place,
A giggling brook, a fluffy face.
A raccoon winks, snatches my snack,
And scampers off, I can't help but laugh back!

The branches sway, they twist and shout,
As I prance around, filled with doubt.
A butterfly flits, then leads me on,
Crafting a path through dusk till dawn.

With every rustle, I'm met with glee,
But watch for twigs that trip over me!
As laughter lingers in the air,
Even the shadows seem to care.

So here I stay, where the fun won't cease,
In nature's arms, I find my peace.
With chuckles shared from leaf to leaf,
A silly dance, my sweet relief.

Wanderers of the Whispering Pines

In the forest, we hear the trees,
Saying, "Don't trip over roots, if you please!"
Squirrels gossip in nutty tones,
While raccoons critique our clumsy moans.

The paths twist and turn like a snake,
Every wrong turn feels like a mistake.
We laugh at our shadows, dancing near,
While a deer gives us a curious leer.

Fungi giggle in colors so bright,
Mushrooms that glow like stars in the night.
With every step, we never feel lost,
Just laughing at nature and the fun it cost.

We stumble on stones, and we leap in streams,
Catching the sunlight and wandering dreams.
As twilight falls, we hear nature's cheer,
Together we wander, there's nothing to fear.

The Hidden Heart of Nature's Maze

In the thickets, there's often a twist,
Did anyone ask the hedgehogs to assist?
We chase after butterflies that wiggle and dart,
While a bush blocks our way, playing its part.

The rabbits plot while we draw our maps,
Pointing at trees and calling them chaps.
A chorus of critters chuckles and caws,
As we bumble onward, ignoring the laws.

With every rustle, we jump and squeal,
Imagining monsters beneath every heel.
But it's just a squirrel with a nut for a crown,
Laughing at us while we tumble down.

Navigating roots that seem to conspire,
As if the forest has feelings of ire.
But in the end, what we truly embrace,
Is the joy of the journey through nature's maze.

Curves of Light and Leafy Grace

Sunlight dapples through branches so green,
As we try to act like we know what we mean.
With elbows knocking and giggles so loud,
Watching the squirrels parade like a crowd.

Leaves rustle softly, whispering secrets,
But we're busy tripping over unseen regrets.
The ferns giggle as we stumble and sway,
Nature's own comedy, directing the play.

We catch glimpses of fairies that flit,
But they split as we take just one little bit.
In our search, we find that laughter's the key,
With every misstep, joy will agree.

So we dance under skies turning pink,
Spinning and laughing, no time to think.
Curves of light, oh, how they embrace,
We're lost in the fun, not the path we face.

In Search of the Enchanted Glade

We set off with snacks in a picnic bag,
Chasing the tales that our friends once bragged.
"Watch out for gnomes!" someone shouts with a grin,
As we march through shadows where mischief begins.

The trees are our buddies on this wild spree,
Rooting for us as they dance with glee.
We dodge and we weave through vines like a race,
All to find that glittery place.

A babbling brook offers a splash or a laugh,
While frogs hold a conference, writing each path.
A rabbit winks, sharing a wink in return,
As we learn that adventure is all we discern.

At last, we arrive at that glade of delight,
Where flowers are blooming, and critters invite.
We plop on the grass, our mission now done,
With snacks in our hands, we bask in the fun.

Chronicles of the Twisting Path

In a forest where the squirrels skitter,
The trees share secrets, but they're quite the quitter.
A deer trips over a root, oh what a sight,
As mushrooms giggle under the soft moonlight.

Rabbits leap with flair, like they're on a stage,
While foxes slyly plot from behind a page.
An owl hoots sharply, but forgot his cue,
While the brook babbles jokes, and the rocks laugh too.

Paths turn and twist like a twisted fairytale,
With shadows that stretch like a cat's lazy tail.
And every creature laughs, quite loud and free,
Chasing away gloom beneath the grand old tree.

So wander through laughter, let every step play,
In nature's own antics, come frolic and sway.
The forest is lively, dressed fancy and bright,
Who knew woodland critters throw parties at night?

Moonlit Musings in the Pines

Beneath all the stars, the pines start to dance,
Squirrels wear sunglasses, taking a chance.
Owls in tuxedos hold a wise debate,
While crickets sip tea, and the world waits with bait.

A raccoon juggles acorns, oh what a show,
And hedgehogs roll dice, in the moon's subtle glow.
Their laughter is vibrant, echoing so sweet,
In this nighttime gala, they frolic on feet.

Moths in long gowns flutter, looking quite grand,
While fireflies twinkle, like a dancing band.
The pines sway gently, like they're tapping their feet,
In this whimsical waltz, they all find their beat.

So come take a stroll as the night unfolds,
In this charming parade, nature's antics are bold.
Each twirl and each giggle serenades the night,
As every creature revels till the dawn's first light.

The Heartbeat of the Forest Floor

In the underbrush, a rabbit sneezes loud,
Scaring a snail who just basked, quite proud.
A dance of the mushrooms, a funny sight,
As beetles shimmy and groove with delight.

Twirling leaves above, whisper tales of cheer,
As ants march to a beat, oh so crystal clear.
A ladybug giggles, stuck in a leaf's fold,
While the groundhog snickers, both shy and bold.

Every rustle and stomp, a comical tune,
In this lively patch, adventures start at noon.
The heartbeat of humor taps softly and quick,
Where echoing laughter makes every joke stick.

From roots deep in earth to the tips up high,
Nature's grown lively, not a single goodbye.
So listen and wander, where the laughs never cease,
In this joyful haven, find your fun and peace.

A Tapestry of Bark and Blossom

A tree wearing bark like a cozy old cloak,
Stands proud and hushed while the bushes just poke.
Blossoms giggle softly, flirting with bees,
As the flowers gossip under the sun with ease.

A crow tries to dance but slips on his wing,
Making the sparrows all laugh, oh what a thing!
While ferns sway gently to the beat of the breeze,
The forest floor echoes with the rustle of leaves.

Sunlight streams down in bright, dappled hues,
And the path twists and turns, giving hints of clues.
With each silly critter and heartwarming sight,
The tale of this grove is pure joy and delight.

So wander through petals, with laughter abound,
Let the nature around you wrap joy all around.
In this tapestry woven by humor and cheer,
The magic of life whispers, "Come dance, my dear!"

Ferns and Fantasies

In the ferns, I see a dance,
A squirrel trying to advance.
He twirls and spins, oh what a sight,
But trips on roots, oh what a fright!

Mushrooms sport their lively hats,
While crickets strum on tiny mats.
A raccoon joins the fun parade,
His clumsy moves a grand charade.

The sun peeks through the leafy crown,
As critters plot to chase me down.
They sting with laughter, full of glee,
While I just wish to roam carefree.

So here I stand, I'll join the show,
With laughter loud, we steal the show.
Amidst the ferns, we find our place,
In nature's dance, a joyous race.

A Reverie Among Ancient Trees

Beneath the boughs, where shadows play,
An ancient oak has much to say.
His branches whisper tales of old,
Of acorns falling, pickled gold.

The squirrels chatter, full of sass,
As they attempt the art of class.
They strut in hats and fancy ties,
While birds roll eyes and just fly by.

I plop beneath the leafy shade,
To join the starlit squirrel parade.
But oh, my sandwich's gone astray,
A thief in fur had made my day!

So here I lounge, so very grand,
In ancient woods, it's just as planned.
With laughter ringing through the trees,
I feel like royalty with ease.

The Enchanted Thicket

In thickets deep, where wild things snooze,
A fox wears shoes, but not the blues.
He prances 'round, a dapper sight,
With twinkling eyes, he steals the night.

A hedge of berries, red and sweet,
Caught a bee who had lost his beat.
He buzzes round, confused, bemused,
Then lands in jam, so overfused!

The owls are hooting, it's a blast,
While rabbits plan a picnic fast.
Yet sandwiches are all just crumbs,
As mulberry stains cause frantic sums!

So let's dance wild in this thicket fun,
Where every day is just a pun.
In nature's joke, we find our niche,
And laugh and frolic, oh what a peach!

Lullabies of the Leafy Realm

In the leafy realm, a lullaby,
The owls croon while crickets sigh.
The trees do sway, like dancers free,
A serenade for you and me.

While chipmunks hum a silly tune,
As fireflies twinkle like a moon.
A badger dreams of flying high,
And snorts awake with a sleepy sigh.

The breeze it giggles, soft and light,
Tickles the leaves, oh what a sight!
A cozy nap beneath the shade,
With dreams of capers unafraid.

So close your eyes, let laughter rise,
In this green world beneath the skies.
With creatures prancing all around,
In lullabies, our joy is found!

The Lace of Light in Leafy Hideaways

In the trees, a playful tease,
Sunlight dances, makes us sneeze.
Squirrels giggle in acorn hats,
While owls hoot, striking silly chats.

Breezes whisper, tickle our toes,
Nature's laughter as wild wind blows.
A rabbit jumps and steals a bite,
From my picnic, oh what a sight!

Mushrooms wear their polka dots,
Like little clowns in tangled knots.
A fox prances, proud and spry,
Chasing shadows, oh my, oh my!

Underneath the leafy sprawl,
We chase fun, we have a ball.
Giggles echo, spirits high,
In this place, we just can't lie.

Secrets of the Subtle Shroud

Beneath the cloak of trees so wide,
Lurks a secret – can't hide!
A chatter of mushrooms too proud,
Whispering tales beneath the cloud.

With lizards winking, mischief planned,
They toss confetti of leafy sand.
Frogs in tuxedos croak a tune,
Under the light of the cheeky moon.

A squirrel slips, oh what a show,
Chasing his tail, he goes too slow.
Beneath ferns, fairies trip and fall,
In this shroud, we frolic and sprawl.

To follow the paths where laughter sways,
Is to discover the forest's plays.
With secrets tucked in each old tree,
Join the dance, come laugh with me!

Canopies of Calm and Curiosity

In leafy canopies, a maze unfolds,
Where even the shyest squirrel scolds.
With branches twisty, it's quite absurd,
The whispers of leaves, oh how they stirred!

A hedgehog's hat looks quite a sight,
As it waddles off into the night.
With giggles echoing from the brook,
Each turn we take gets another look!

A shy rabbit with big round eyes,
Hiding from surprise in a pile of fries.
The crickets croon, a band so sweet,
Making melodies with tiny feet.

Beneath the arch of branches twined,
Curiosity, oh how it grinds!
Let's skip through this green-glade glee,
Our laughter joins the rustling spree.

The Murmurs of Mossy Memories

In a quiet nook, where moss does dwell,
Old stories linger, can you tell?
A snail on a journey, slow and grand,
Leaves a trail like a silver strand.

Fungi gather for a tea party,
Chatting about their fungi hearty.
The mushrooms gossip, the toads just sigh,
Under a blanket of clouds floating high.

An ant with a suitcase calls a road,
While daisies tickle, their blossoms glowed.
"Where to?" shouts, "I'm off to the fair!"
As ladybugs join without a care!

So let's roam where the soft moss lies,
And find the laugh that never dies.
In these corners where whispers fade,
We'll craft tales that never trade.

Forgotten Trails and Timeless Tales

In the woods where no one goes,
The squirrels tell jokes, who knows?
They giggle and scamper, tails in flight,
While dodging the leaves that flutter to fright.

A lost hiker claims he found a way,
But tripped on roots that chose to stay.
His map was drawn by a raccoon's paws,
Now his friends are laughing, with very loud guffaws.

The owls hoot a rhythm, quite absurd,
As rabbits compose the sweetest word.
Their melody echoes, a nutty refrain,
Sending giggles up and down the lane.

So if you wander, take heed of the fun,
The trees have secrets, and laughter's begun.
In the heart of the thicket, stories unfold,
If you listen closely, they'll never grow old.

The Song of the Swaying Boughs

The branches dance to a tune offbeat,
With feathered friends tapping their happy feet.
A raccoon leads with a wild two-step,
While the deer just stop and take a pep rep.

The pine cones tumble, causing a fuss,
As critters all gather, creating a bus.
The frogs croak a chorus, loud and crude,
While the trees sway along, not a hint of rude.

Squirrels join in, flipping with glee,
Singing about snacks, wild and free.
Every rustle and shake brings chuckles anew,
In this wacky place where laughter just grew.

So grab your friends, and follow their lead,
Every bough holds a giggle, a sprinkle of creed.
In this forest of joy, dance like the breeze,
For the song of the boughs brings a sense of ease.

Beneath the Boughs of Eternity

Under the branches, the shadows do play,
Where mischief abounds every single day.
The raccoons prank with a splash and a dive,
And the porcupines chuckle, feeling alive.

In a patch of sunlight, a bear tries to tan,
But the bees buzz around, devising a plan.
He swats at their humor, arms flailing with cheer,
Only to slip and land right in the smear.

The foxes, so clever, throw parties at night,
With glowworm lanterns, a sparkling sight.
But the owls hoot warnings, "You've stepped on my toes!"
While the hedgehogs sneak snacks, in joke-laden prose.

So nestle right here, in this joyful sphere,
Where giggles and chuckles replace all your fear.
For beneath the boughs, life's always a joke,
In the echo of laughter, the enchantment awoke.

Moondust in the Moss

Moonlight drips on the velvety green,
As fireflies twinkle, a magical scene.
A lost little mushroom starts telling a tale,
Of how it sat waiting, while others set sail.

The rabbits decide it's the best time to play,
With leaps and bounds in a silvery sway.
But who should they bump into, it's a hare, quite daft,
Who tripped on a toadstool, and away he laughed.

The shadows are giggling, the leaves are aflame,
As the moonbeams tickle, calling each name.
"Dance on the moss, let your worries all fly,
For tomorrow we'll hide from the watchful eye."

So gather your dreams, let the fun take its course,
Under stars and whispers, we'll unleash our force.
With moondust a-sparkle, we'll giggle and prance,
In a world full of wonder, let's embrace the chance.

In Pursuit of the Untamed

In the forest I tripped over a log,
Chasing squirrels, they called me a hog.
I slipped in the mud, not quite like a pro,
Fingers all sticky, with honey on toe.

The trees chuckled softly, swaying with glee,
As I danced like a fool, wild and free.
With branches as partners, I twirled all around,
Voice of the owls shouted, 'Hey, keep it down!'

I found a lost shoe, who knows where it went?
A raccoon borrowed it, that's my best guess.
I wandered in circles, but isn't it fun?
With laughter and nature, I felt like the one.

A deer with a bowtie offered a snack,
'Try these berries! They're quite the whack!'
I took a big bite, and oh what a taste—
My dance moves came back, I picked up the pace!

A frog joined the tango, leaping so high,
"Can you match my jumps? Give it a try!"
In the chase for the wild, I've lost track of time,
But with friends in the forest, life's always a rhyme.

Whispers of the Wandering Wind

The whispers of breezes tease the tall grass,
They giggle and gush as I stumble and pass.
I tangled my hair in the twirling spree,
Each gust of the wind loves to laugh at me!

A butterfly joined, it seemed quite a sight,
Danced on my nose, gave my cheeks a fright!
I waved it along with a twirl of my hat,
"Hey, where are you going? Don't leave just like that!"

The tall pine trees leaned in for a chat,
With gossip and secrets, oh what a spat!
I swayed with the flowers, in a giggle-spree,
The daisies all whispered, "Come dance with me!"

But watch out for thorns that might ruin the cheer,
Each step that I take seems to bring me near,
To prickly reminders of nature's own jest,
A poke here and there—oh, it's all for the best!

As daylight retreats, I'll stumble back home,
With laughter and tales of my frolics to comb.
Among trees and the wind, the funny times blend,
In the dance of the wild, where chuckles don't end!

Shadows that Sing of Solitude

In the hush of trees, I trip and sway,
Where shadow-critters plot all day.
A squirrel giggles, 'What a sight!'
As I tumble down, oh what a fright!

The deer roll eyes, like they're the kings,
While I'm lost in laughter, tripping on springs.
Each rustle whispers, 'Should we laugh too?'
'They're only human, what can they do?'

A fox takes bets on my next big fall,
While I try to be graceful, not trip at all.
The trees all chuckle with a rustling cheer,
'Don't worry, dear friend, we all have our year!'

So I dance with the shadows, prance with glee,
In this leafy circus, come join me!
Let's sway with the breeze, we'll be the show,
In a forest where laughter is free to flow.

A Festival of Ferns and Fragrance

Ferns wear tiaras of dewdrops bright,
Throwing a party under the moonlight.
The daisies bring snacks, and the bees hum a tune,
While I twirl with my pals, under the glowing moon!

Mushrooms in tuxedos, all set to dance,
Prancing around like they've lost their chance.
'Come join the fun!,' the tall pines decree,
'Even the stars want a peek, come see!'

The flowers are gossiping, whispering sneers,
About the old oak who forgot his gears.
As he shimmies and shakes, stumbling quite wide,
We all erupt in laughter, his woodsy pride!

At this fragrant soirée, with each little twirl,
We celebrate nature's most whimsical whirl.
With a wink to the moon, we'll dance till it's late,
In the festival of ferns, we just can't wait!

The Spirit of the Hidden Grove

In a grove where giggles rustle like leaves,
The old tree stands tall, while mischief it weaves.
'Let's play hide and seek,' whispers a breeze,
But the trees need a nap; they're bringing me to my knees!

Branches stretch out, like they want to run,
While I chase shadows, oh what fun!
A chipmunk yells, 'Catch me if you dare!'
But I step on a twig, and fall with a flare!

The spirit of the grove cracks a hearty laugh,
As I wrestle with roots on this nature path.
'Worry not, dear friend,' says a wise old pine,
'In a world of woodlands, we all intertwine!'

So I rise up again, dust off the leaves,
With a grin that says, 'I'm not one to grieve.'
Together we frolic, the trees and I,
In this secretive realm, where we all can fly!

Through the Needle's Eye of Trees

Through the needle's eye where the sunlight splays,
I wander through quirks of nature's displays.
A rabbit hops by with a wink and a nod,
As I tumble and roll, looking a bit odd!

The whispers of the leaves tease my shoes,
'Careful now, friend, don't sing the blues!'
Elusive and merry, the critters take flight,
While I'm busy laughing, what a comical sight!

A sparrow serenades from a branch overhead,
'Look at that human, full of dread!'
But with every misstep and chuckle I share,
I find joy in this chaos, without a care!

So onward I go, on this zany spree,
Through the needle's eye where I can be free.
With laughter as my compass, I dance through the trees,
In this frolicsome forest, where I feel the ease!

Sylvan Reflections

In the forest, squirrels plot,
While rabbits dance and twirl a lot.
A bear trips over a fallen log,
Chasing his dreams, or maybe a frog.

The owls hoot with all their might,
While deer are having quite a fright.
Trees gossip about the days of yore,
It's a charm-filled wood, who could ask for more?

What's that rustle? A fox in a hat?
He flips his tail, imagine that!
A raccoon's stealing snacks with flair,
Painting his face like a true debonair.

Amongst the laughter, a whispering breeze,
Tickles the ferns and dances the leaves.
Nature's a jester, with tricks up her sleeve,
In this joyous realm, who wouldn't believe?

Petals on the Pine-Scented Breeze

Bumblebees buzz in a playful race,
While flowers giggle, keeping pace.
A gentleman toad hops up too high,
With dreams of catching a butterfly.

Pine trees sway, wearing crowns with pride,
A squirrel in shades, what a sight outside!
Nature throws a party, come take a seat,
Join the critters for a dance so sweet.

The sun peeks down through a leafy screen,
Tickling the ferns that giggle and preen.
A hedgehog joins, thinking he's suave,
But tripping over roots, oh such a laugh!

With petals fluttering like confetti fall,
The forest shouts, "Come one, come all!"
In this joyous carnival, spirits soar,
Adventure awaits behind every door!

Twilit Tangles

The evening falls with shadows long,
Frogs perform their twilight song.
Mice are giggling in a crooked line,
Chasing their tails, isn't it divine?

A moonlit path paved by fireflies,
Dancing up high in the velvet skies.
And what's that sound? A clumsy chime,
A racoon's mistake, oh what a time!

Hedgehogs huddle for a warm embrace,
While owls debate about the best race.
With mischief abound, it's a sight to see,
In twilit tangles, there's no decree.

The wind whispers secrets, soft and clear,
Giggling leaves fill the air with cheer.
So let us wander 'neath the stars so bright,
In this tangled wood, it feels just right!

A Tapestry of Trunks

In trunks of trees, stories grow,
Of cheeky critters and rivers that flow.
A Badger in glasses reads a smart book,
While a squirrel critiques with a puzzled look.

Branches twist like pretzel rods,
As branches sway, giving high-fives to gods.
A crow caws loudly, thinking he's wise,
While a fox teaches him how to improvise.

Through the leaves, the sunbeams play,
Casting shadows that dance all day.
Toe-tapping tunes on acorn drums,
The forest folk sing till morning comes.

A tapestry woven with laughter and fun,
In every nook, there's a tale to run.
Step right up, and join the spree,
In this cheerful wood, so wild and free!

Whispers in the Canopy

Squirrels plotting in the trees,
Chasing shadows on the breeze.
Joking leaves that dance and sway,
Tell me secrets of the day.

Bumblebees in goofy flight,
Buzzing tales 'til late at night.
Worms in line for the worm parade,
Frogs in tuxedos serenade.

Mushrooms giggle, roots conspire,
Bark is laughing at the fire.
While owls wink with knowing glances,
In this realm of leafy dances.

Chipmunks sharing silly pranks,
Rolling acorns past the banks.
In this forest, full of cheer,
Nature's jesters always near.

Beneath the Leafy Veil

Dancing on the forest floor,
Turtles racing, hear them roar!
Bunnies hop and make a fuss,
While the hedgehog rides the bus.

Shadows flicker, branches sway,
Trees are giggling, come what may.
Squirrels play their nutty games,
While owls hoot their silly names.

Fungi sport their polka dots,
Moths in capes, oh what a lot!
Every critter dressed so odd,
In this realm, they're all a god!

Sunlight filters through the green,
Making mischief, quite the scene.
With every rustle, every call,
The forest laughs and shares it all.

Secrets of the Forest Floor

Ants on a mission, marching tight,
Some lost their snacks, oh what a fright!
Rabbits tell their tall, tall tales,
While the snail drinks from tiny pails.

Mice are dancing on a log,
While crickets play the favorite frog.
A shadow leaps—a playful tease,
Wandering through the leafy seas.

Beneath the layers of fallen leaves,
Lies the magic, oh what it weaves!
Earthworms smile, their tricks galore,
In this forest, there's never a bore.

With every rustle, giggles soar,
Nature's jesters, always more.
Secrets scattered wild and free,
In this forest, joy's decree!

The Pathless Grove

Lost in echoes of delight,
Bouncing squirrels take to flight.
Napping bears with funny dreams,
Chasing moonbeams, or so it seems.

Wandering down the pathless way,
Finding treasures in disarray.
Frogs in hats, a merry band,
Making music across the land.

Trees wear coats of bark so bright,
Mocking shadows in the night.
Every gust of wind that blows,
Sings the songs that nobody knows.

In this grove, laughter shines,
With every twist in twisted vines.
Join the dance, and lose your way,
In this jolly, wild display!

The Gentle Tug of Nature's Call

In the woods, my shoes do squeak,
Chasing squirrels, my knees go weak.
Branches wave, as if to say,
"Join the dance, just lose your way!"

A frog jumps high, I trip and fall,
"What a splash!" I laugh, enthralled.
A ladybug gives me a wink,
As I pause to sip and think.

The trees conspire in hidden jest,
To put my patience to the test.
A breeze tickles my funny bone,
Whispers secrets to me alone!

Amidst the rustle and the glee,
Even thorns seem to agree.
Life's a riddle, dark and bright,
In nature's laugh, I find my light.

The Breezes that Carry Dreams

Whimsical winds dance through the trees,
Tickling my hair like a playful tease.
A gnome poses, all green and stout,
With a cheeky grin, he shouts, "Let's out!"

Clouds float by on a sweet charade,
Are they lost? Or just afraid?
A squirrel scolds, its cheeks all stuffed,
"Quit your giggles! Enough's enough!"

A butterfly in polka-dot pants,
Flutters by, inviting prance.
I attempt a clumsy pirouette,
And tumble down—oh, not my best!

A stream sings tunes that make me grin,
As fish all giggle, their scales a-spin.
Together we laugh, both furry and fine,
In this funny realm, where spirits entwine!

Pathways of Wonder in the Green

Every path opens arms so wide,
In the embrace of the forest, I glide.
A tree says, "Why not take a seat?"
But watch your step—there's mud at your feet!

A signpost stands with a cheeky grin,
Pointing to nowhere, let the fun begin!
A rabbit hops by with a jaunty flip,
"Join my race, or stay, and trip!"

Mushrooms giggle with tangled roots,
Dancing shadows, in grand pursuits.
A twig snaps loud, a startled crow,
Caws in laughter, "Now, where'd that go?"

With every turn, the woods conspire,
To tickle my toes and set my heart higher.
Nature's jesters, in twirls and leaps,
In this grand stage, fun never sleeps!

The Poetry of Pine and Petal

Pine trees whisper secrets low,
While petals giggle, putting on a show.
A toad croaks verses, deep and wise,
Just as the sun peeks through the skies.

Underfoot, a carpet of leaves,
Join the chorus of nature's sleeves.
An owl overly dramatic hoots,
"This scene deserves some fancy boots!"

With snickers shared from every glen,
Even an acorn joins the pen.
Each branch a stanza, each root a rhyme,
Together they plot, just killing time!

In this poetry, laughter reigns,
Amidst shadows and sunny lanes.
So take a glance at this forest mint,
And smile—life's a joke that won't ever stint!

www.ingramcontent.com/pod-product-compliance
Lightning Source LLC
Chambersburg PA
CBHW071838160426
43209CB00003B/346